SAX BURGLAR BLUES

*for my father and in memory of my mother,
inspirational both*

SAX BURGLAR BLUES

Robert Walton

SEREN

Seren is the book imprint of
Poetry Wales Press Ltd.
57 Nolton Street, Bridgend, Wales, CF31 3AE
www.serenbooks.com
facebook.com/SerenBooks
twitter@SerenBooks

The right of Robert Walton to be identified as
the author of this work has been asserted in accordance
with the Copyright, Designs and Patents Act, 1988.

ISBN: 978-1-78172-408-8
ebook: 978-1-78172-412-5
Kindle: 978-1-78172-416-3

A CIP record for this title is available from the British Library.

The publisher acknowledges the financial assistance of the Welsh Books Council.

Cover Artwork: JEFF SCHLANGER, musicWitness® 2017
SAX Burglar (Joe McPhee Solo) — Original art 40 x 27.5" made Live @ Brecht
Forum, New York City, January 29, 2000.
www.musicwitness.com

Printed by Airdrie Print Services Ltd.

Contents

Man with a Double Bass on his Back

What kind of hump-backed, giant-mandibled creature is this
when the city's locked in its mid-week mid-day business –

buses crammed in their bays, cars jamming the street,
pedestrians paused at the crossing, waiting for the green –

and here he comes, all tensile legs and fleet-of-foot intent,
this armour-plated coleoptera bent beneath his instrument?

He weaves his way among them as if he's followed
a labyrinth of string and risen from the underworld,

rehearsing the captive beasts in his head. The subterranean
Mingus rumble of his bow driving to and fro. The Haden

pizzicatos plucked like hooves across the frets.
The Scott LaFaro melodies exhaling bestial breath

between the bridge and scroll. And lo, the thorax-swinging
jazz scarab is loose in the streets and no-one's looking.

O dung-scavenger, o burdened, carapacial death-watch,
they avert their eyes at their peril when you're at large.

Ironing

The white cotton handkerchief, pressed
creaseless, heat in its fibres and folded
in half, edge aligned to edge,

is the dance-card my mother holds and presses
again, with the blue embroidered R
in the corner the only name on the list.

She adds it to the pile of his vests, socks
and pants, turns and steps in time
to a waltz as she lifts his crumpled shirt

from the basket and hums along to the tune
on the radio, hips swaying, legs
partnering the X of the board.

She holds it close in her arms, sleeves
stretched, and lays it down, smoothes it
flat under the warmth of her hands.

Twm Siôn Cati

In Mrs Jones' class, the chairs became
rocky outcrops he hid behind to surprise
his victims on the upland route between
the door and window. A table in the corner
was an ironmonger's store in Llandovery
where he pulled a fast one with a pot;
and draped with a blanket, the cave on Dinas Hill
where he took his refuge was magicked up.
With rolled-up sleeves and cardi hanging loose,
she told us where to stand and how to say
our lines as if she were Twm the highwayman
himself issuing commands. We'd chant the chorus
to the stamp of her shoe on the parquet floor.
When she held a finger to her lips, there was hush.
When she called us out by name, we'd cower or glow.
To wear the cloak and hat she'd brought from home,
we stood up straight with bulging chests and hands
clasped tight behind our backs to catch her eye.
To sit on teacher's chair and the soft embroidered
cushion that were his horse and saddle as he galloped
away beyond the rule of law, we thrust
our hands up high to be her choice. Those winter
afternoons, when she stood at the front of the room,
wiry-haired, fierce-eyed, her words
were red kites playing the thermals over the Teifi.

Cyfri'r Geifr: Counting the Goats

a traditional Welsh folk song

With the tip of the twelve-inch rule she uses
to name the countries and capital cities
on a map of the world, or beat the rhythm
of the times-tables we chant before assembly,

Mrs Jones points to the words
in coloured chalk on the board
and the goats of the song are *wen, ddu,
goch* and *las* because we sing them so.

Their lips and flanks and docked tails
are whiter than the snow on Snowdon,
blacker than a witch's cauldron,
redder than a dragon's blood

or bluer than a kingfisher's breast
because she tells us so at the end
of the day when we leave our desks and sit
at her feet in a circle for story-time –

and she taps her shiny buckled shoe
to the tempo we sing, a slow, exact
pronunciation of notes and syllables
at first, then faster, faster, faster

with each refrain as we chase the goats
down the hill through bracken and gulley
and count them safely into the pens
of our minds in Bryn Hafod. And years later,

when I scramble over those tumbledown drystone
consonants, squeeze those vowels
and diphthongs between tongue and teeth,
I hear the bells tinkling on distant slopes

and watch them running from crag to ridge —
wen, ddu, goch and *las*
gafr wen, wen wen
gafr ddu, ddu, ddu
gafr goch, goch, goch
gafr las, las, las
and binc.

Man and Boy

I wait for the waft of tobacco on the other side
of the door to grow stronger, for the brass knob
above my head to turn. The panel's varnished
grain is a giant's fingerprint. I clutch
The Dandy to my chest like a parchment scroll.

First you offer me Korky the Cat's green eyes
and shiny nose. Flick past Hungry Horace
and Plum Macduff; skip the chunky chin
of Desperate Dan. You hold your grandson
on your knee the way you never held your daughter.

Your Granite City voice is soft on my neck:
Black Bob the loyal Border Collie scents
the trail and leads the rescue. Frame by frame
your finger points as he leaps across the hills
to the crofter stranded in her snowbound house.

And while the dog gazes into his master's eyes,
you close the comic, enclose me in your arms.

Up the Bluebirds!

for my father

Season on season, week on week,
your irrepressible optimism on the phone:
down the line I hear the chant
of the home crowd, see the pitch
where the ball arcs between boot and upright
or hangs in the wind over upturned heads.
And yes, I try to share that surge
of joy as the net bulges and you leap
from your seat, arms upthrust, to roar
for the goals that justify your lifelong fervour.

Week in week out, each word you speak –
the keeper's saves, the striker's misses,
the names of players I've never heard of,
the tactics, the ref's outrageous decisions –
spins from your mouth like a string
of bright rosettes in some conjuring trick.
I listen, ask questions, enthuse.
Somewhere in a wardrobe in my house
a Bluebirds scarf, bought years ago outside
the ground, lies folded in the dark.

Cataracts

Mornings, she tends her garden in the sky:
plastic sheeting wired to the rails
ten floors up – her balcony hothouse.

Hairy knobbles, wobbly perpen-
diculars, bristly plumps of flesh,
the cacti proliferate as her vision

declines. But nothing passes scrutiny:
the overnight speck on a stem, a brown tip
crinkling the green leather.

In pots and gravel-trays, she propagates
the mammillaria, golden barrels,
bunny-ears and bishop's caps

with her instrument of nurture: a single
blade that cuts the thick skin
and nicks the tender sponge within.

The Old Medicine

The only medication
your doctor prescribes
at this late stage – a bottle
of Guinness. It glows

on your bedside table, Nanna,
a devotional lamp
for your nightly round of the Duke,
the Vic and the Clive,

your local Magh Meall
where you'll leap to the table
for a rousing rebel-song
and a knees-up jig

that gets you barred each time
until you return
with a joke, a fag and a promise
you'll never keep.

You can't resist that ring
of froth at the cap,
the double refraction of ruby
stout and vitreous brown,

the call to arms of the amber
oval label
with Arthur's ornate
signature and harp.

So take it, Nanna: grasp
the neck and swig it
down, that roasted barley brew,
your final toast.

Grancha

Step into this room and you'll find him in the far
corner in his old wooden armchair between
the black-lead range where the kettle's always steaming
and the curtainless window looking out onto the yard.

His vantage-point. The fifty years he lived here,
the fifty years since. Left leg cocked over
one arm of the chair, the tilt of his bulk along
the polished length of the other. He takes it all in.

The grandchildren playing touch out the back. The click
of the latch, the wait and the flush in the outside toilet.
The fluster of pigeons released from the Harveys' loft;
their solo return in fading afternoon light.

In this room, he's a lopsided Buddha who casts
his gaze on all who come and go. As if
he's hunkered down in pads and gloves behind
the stumps in Thompson's Park, niggling the batsmen

back to the pavilion. As if he's still on guard
at the rear of a train in Cardiff General, running
his eye along the platform, whistle to his lips,
counting the seconds for the signal to depart.

Greenland

This endless whiteness, how far does it stretch?
This bolt of satin, this sheet of cremfilm unfurled?

Greater, from this height, than any snowbound steppe;
from this proximity, deeper than any precipice of cloud.

Look for a vein of blue, you'll never find it. A blotch
of pink or red in the skin – not a trace.

A heart of ice, no give and take. To read
the future in its stillness is to dream of cryonics.

I wish it any colour other than white – a play
of shadow at least, its flatness puckered, creased.

It's a head on the shoulders of the globe, the ocean
swirling round it, a gown that should lend it grace.

It's a head at rest on a pillow and I'm willing my mother's
eyes to open. I'm looking for a flicker of green.

Fall

Not from any great height – not a running jump you'd take
at the pool, staccato steps to the tip of the board, the bounce into
a jack-knife dive, slicing the surface in a splash of blue bravado

and not the final three deep breaths a hundred feet up on
the ledge, arms outstretched in cruciform silhouette before the leap,
the yell of release and the spiral plunge down the umbilical bungee –

no, this is from standing, both feet square on the ground and not
as when the legs wobble at the top of a ladder in a moment of panic
and you grasp the rungs in a slapstick clatter of gasps and aluminium

nor the stairwell tumble, half-way down, that happens to a child
and will in your dotage, limbs askew and every disc in the spine
hitting the treads, a bump-bump-bump of timber rattling bone –

this is not a fall from grace or fame; not from some moral summit;
no Faustian pact, misjudged from the start, too late to repent its impact;
no scatter-fire of light from Lucifer's armies storming the night.

No, this is the step across the room towards the door, on the level,
the homo erectus evolution of balance and motion from toe to hip
to neck and cranium, the repertoire of ligaments, nerves and muscle,

when one leg gives. Crumples. A blur of things being where they should
not be. Floor rising. Ceiling flying. Horizons aslant. And the body
capsizes beneath a wave, firing its flare before the vessel goes down.

A Bus Named Dusty

Swings into view on the bend outside Brighton Station
and races down North Street, swaying on its tyres with a glint
of blonde and cherry livery like a swish of hair, a hint of lips,
and sashays through the afternoon sunlight, raising an arm
with a flick of the wrist to summon the honky brass beat
of *Can I Get A Witness? – Witness, Witness!*
then bears down past the kebab-and-burger bar, the windscreen
gleaming, reflecting the scud of clouds across the sky
as if the cymbals were already crashing out behind the chorus
of *When the Lovelight Starts Shining Through His Eyes,*
and in a grin of defiance shoots across the lights just before
the segue into *You Don't Own Me,* eyes closing into thick mascara,
head dropping to a wistful tilt as the tempo slows,
drawing in now to the kerb with a shush of brakes
and the door opening, a breath taken in the final whispered notes
of *Will You Still Love Me Tomorrow?*

POETRY LIBRARY

Sax Burglar Blues

As he crept through the darkness to ease
    you from the stand where you sat
like a swan in the reeds – could he hear
    your stabs and riffs, fierce
and rhythmic as wings beating the waters,
    rising into the groove of the air?

And when he touched you, hand-in-glove
    fumbling your gleaming mechanisms,
your keys clumping in his grasp
    – did he hear your screech
of protest, the upper octave alarm
    of a hawk squalling on the leash?

He took you apart. Dismantled note
    from note your smooth arpeggios,
your bebop solos. Squeezed the bell
    beneath his arm. Twisted
out the crook. Slipped the mouthpiece
    from the cork. And stooping

to zip you piece by piece into the bag,
    did he share the night-owl
haunts of your rambling blues? Could he
    imagine your bottom B flat,
profound and plaintive enough to rouse
    a seal from the ocean depths?

Three out of Four Original Members

To look at me then and now you'd never think
I cut that twelve-bar riff in a single take.
Tommy stuck the demo in the can and said
we had it made. We chucked our jobs and took
the rock'n'roll A to Z from Aberdare
to Aberdeen and down to Ashby-de-la-Zouch,
crammed in the van on a make-or-break trip:
sleeping-bags, spliffs, two's-ups, farts
and back-stage scraps. At three in the morning
in Toddington Services, Gavin dunked his burger
in my coffee once too often. I never wore
those orange loons and Afghan coat again.
Never touched my Fender Strat. The dep
they picked up knew my solo off by heart,
its swampy bottleneck chords in overdrive,
that tingling tremolo flattened seventh.
One-hit wonders. Doesn't stop them touring
their Greatest Hits album thirty years
down the road. Even Whispering Bob
admits on the *Old Grey Whistle Test* archive,
he plays that lick on air-guitar in the shower.

The Poet of the Mason's Arms

i.m. John Tripp, 1927–86

With glass in hand and ash that never falls from your fag,
you work the punters in the bar with your peregrine eye
like an evangelist touting Gideon Bibles in North Korea,
you curmudgeon, you *outsider in worn corduroy*,

you farrier's son who knows nothing about horses and less
than nothing about the workings of the internal combustion engine
but that doesn't stop you picking a dead-cert accumulator
at Aintree from Charley-in-the-Corner's 'Racing Post'

or telling Tony the Taxi why his latest fleet of customised cabs
are Noddy-cars with knobs-on. And as for Dave the barman,
what meat to sink your teeth into, fresh from Trinity Cambridge
with First Class Honours in Maths: you challenge him to prove

Fermat's Last Theorem in the time it takes to burn a match
then argue the toss about the price of a Peter's Pie and a pint.

When all is said and done, one by one you take them to task,
shake hands and take them to heart on your incendiary shift,
slip away to sit alone behind the stop-tap lock-in doors
of the lounge, sink into a plush armchair in the quiet afternoon

and open your book, your mind attuned to the voices gathering
at the edge of the page. Your cider stands on its mat in the sunlight,
a golden crystal-ball whose mists are clearing, and they come
to you, your sprite companions, your inheritance file of ghosts:

Rimbaud, Beckett, Bukowski, Shirley Temple and Bogart,
David Jones, Gwenallt, Jack the Lion from Rhiwbina,
Taffy the Terrier, the family doctor with Scotch on his breath,
Miss Roberts, and Gwyn and Griff the boys from the Bargoed terrace,

crowding in and whispering, loading your pen with its vaccine
against the eastern zones. Here in Eglwys Newydd,
John, you give no quarter to *the grubbing merchants of cant*
while you wait for that visa to Tongwynlais, a mile up the road.

Sole Bystander as the Convoy Passes

Nelson Mandela, Brighton, September 2000

The wave he gave through the window
of the limousine as it cruised along
the promenade in bright sunshine

– it might have closed into a solid fist
held high on a triumphant arm
as if it gripped a stick of dynamite

or it might have twisted at the wrist
and offered a hand for me to clasp
and shake, our lifelines intertwined

like rivers on a map meeting at
the estuary, like tales from distant lands
that find their roots in familiar soil

– but it was an arm that slowly rose
like a swimmer's from the sea,
the palm and fingers cupped to catch

the water on the downward stroke,
powering forward; it was a hand
that was a bird perched on a branch

waiting for the moment to fly free.

Invigilation

i.m. Seamus Heaney, 1939–2013

As I strolled the aisles beneath the glare and hum
of fluorescent light in the examination-hall,
the heads were down, the candidates hunch-backed
over their scripts, when I came across one

who'd given up on his five-hundred words analysis
of imagery in *Digging* and *The Early Purges* to busy
himself instead with drawing a pair of devil's horns
and lascivious goatee-beard on your photograph

printed in the anthology. The lad applied himself
with monkish dedication to the diabolic effect
each pencil-stroke imposed on your face
with its rainy-sky gaze, its grainy complexion,

and I thought that if those lips of yours could speak
they'd tell the novice artist he'd caught you in the act
for in the art of poetry the devil is in the detail, or
on this occasion, the detail was in the devil. I watched

your eyebrows thicken and grizzle, your cheeks shrink,
rakish as Rasputin. All those lessons he'd slumped
at his desk, ploughing through metaphors, churning up
the assonance, the Anglo-Saxon alliteration:

he held their necks between his finger and his thumb
like kittens he'd toss into a bucket, *the scraggy wee shits*,
and sluice them down until they drowned. And here
you are, ever vigilant, coming up at his shoulder

some twenty years away, the wraith of a voice
he never heard. You speak with the soil of Bellaghy
in your mouth, urging him on in his purgatory until
the end of the test, when the pencil's laid to rest.

Reader

Squeezing the fibres
of each letter
his finger prods –
as if at any moment

the stems and curves
might turn tail
and slip away,
unutterable – he holds

his breath, twists
his tongue around
the root of a sound
and mouths a scramble

of plosives. Deep
in the labyrinth
of his head, he hears
the snuffle in the dark

until the whisper becomes
a rumble, an echoing
tremor. As he pulls
at the thread, the word

on the tip of his lips roars.

Closing Down

Clutching the change from my tenner in his hand,
the bookshop assistant waits for the till to print
a receipt. I draw a pistol from my pocket, point
its double-fingered barrel in his direction.
'How dare you give me seventy-five per cent
discount? This is sheer daylight robbery!'
I tap the book on the counter – the creaseless
spine, the blue and crimson Roman font
of its title and author's name, the grey jacket
with the ff logo in the corner, those layered pages.
He stares beyond me to the shelves with their lone
remainders aslant on the racks of veneer, vacant
as cavities in the mouth of a customer-service smile.
'Why do you intend to give me change?' I protest
with a glance at the note and coins in the palm of his hand:
'Why not charge me twice or thrice the retail price?
Do you value it so cheaply, this surplus unit
of stock, this hanger-on, this bin-end snip?'
I turn to the customers in the queue for moral
support. Heads down, silent, they calculate
their bargains. The assistant tears the receipt from its roll,
slips it into the bag with the book and slides
my purchase towards me. My pistol folds into a grip
and I nestle the parcel under my arm. My final
look says, The deal is done but I promise you this:
I'll cherish this book; I'll read every word slow
as a brass snail; I'll turn its pages like sheets
of beaten gold. And his nod says, 'I know'.

Ripple

The slice of apple wedged between the bars
is turning brown. Motionless the swing.
On his perch below, my canary has stopped
singing. Head cocked and bill shut tight,
he listens to the silence of his own making.

In markets in Rio, Bangkok, Tenerife
a yellow wave stirs. Canaries stare
at the space beyond confinement. Their eyes
are laser-beams splitting molecules.
The wires of every cage dissolve.

My canary puffs his little chest out,
a golden planet. When his wings unfold,
a feather falls, ripples the water
in his bath – distorts the bright reflection
as his legs stretch and he prepares to leave.

Joey in the Mirror

Not such a chipper chappy, he thinks,
not so chirpy this morning, chum.
Even as he tilts his head
at twenty three degrees from vertical,
first to the left to inspect the tuft
concealing his ear, then to the right
to study the plush of his gorgeous
throat, the world is still askew.
Not a feather out of place,
the vanes and barbs preened perfect
as the weft of a Persian rug.

Yet something in the air persists.
The cusp of a question hangs like the perch
his claws clasp. *I want to sing of
sesame and grass, I want
to sing of figs and sun.* He gazes
at the glass, the blue plastic curve
of its frame, its certain reflection:
millet-spray behind his shoulder,
cuttlebone clipped to the bars.
When he opens his bill, a single silent
note is wedged in the gap.

Anatomia Josephi

Pluck out every feather, from crown to wing
to rump: a golden snowstorm of chemical toxin.

Peel away my skin in strips and weave
a web of plastic, translucent beneath the waves.

Slash the trunks of my muscles one by one,
clear the forest, the smoking plumage of the Amazon.

Squeeze the blood from my heart, my arteries and veins:
blue to red the explosion, the whale, the ocean.

Dismantle the architecture of my honeycomb bones
and dust will turn to sand as the deserts expand.

Snap my furcular, wish for whatever you will:
from its silent rig, my song rises still.

Joey for President

I've hardly taken to my perch
in the oval room of the cage
when they're whispering at the bars,
offering fresh cuttlefish
to sharpen my bill, secret
nocturnal visits from hens
with eyes lustrous as bullets.

Mr President, sir, they say –
checking the windows are sealed –
come out and see the world.
Cut a deal on millet
harvests. Raid the supplies
of canary grass. Splatter
your droppings far and wide.

The liberty bell tinkles
and the door is open, but I won't
be tempted. My song will be
mysterious as the music
of the spheres. Flitting from perch
to swing, my wings unfurl
a flag of stars and plumage.

Croc in the Dock

Beast of Bristol resurfaces with fourth snap of 'crocodile'
The Guardian, 26.06.14

They laugh it off, my lurking shadow, shifting wakeless
just below the surface, my log-snout nuzzling into the flow.
I'm a weary bus-driver's day-dream of Captain Hook,
a hyper-oxygenated jogger's hallucination. They study
the photo's pixelated print to coin a punning caption
and write me off: a hoax to hit the local headlines,
a column-filler that hikes the Likes on *Huffington Post*.
Is it my breath they avoid, the reek of flesh between
my teeth, the leeches at my gums? Or the minus signs
of my eyes, these slits in the skin of creation? Behind
the lock-gates, I wait, tight as a bullet in its chamber.
I can sense a footstep at a thousand metres, a raindrop
fleck a leaf in the canopy. As the water-level rises,
I'm ready to prowl the streets and put the record straight.

Where

St Peter's Church, Castle Park, Bristol

Where a knurled door should let the light edge into shadow
       with a clunk of its latch and hinges creaking,
the gate is locked, keyless, its iron grille barring the vision.

Where the font should sit – the sculpted octagon
       of its bowl offering its watermark –
no trace of its signature, no print of its pedestal's bulk.

Where the pews should reach across the nave
       with paperchain silhouettes hunched in prayer:
no furniture, no flesh, an aisle of absence.

Where the eighteen arches should raise their columns
       to trim capitals, voussoirs, keystones:
bodged concrete casing, roughcast in-fill, raw brickwork.

Where the altar-rail should draw a line of sanctuary
       inviolable in stone, wood, marble:
groundsel, bittercress, willowherb creep through cracked slabs.

Where the roof should be, its curved geometry
       of ribs and vaulting making sockets for the eyes:
the sky's a blue memory of wings flying in.

The tower remains intact: its pinnacles and crenellation,
       its gargoyles staring out the time to come.
Inside, a bell that never tolls, is never silent.

Incident at Birdcage Walk

She'll never make it to the end of the cracked-paving path
she's approaching in those poppy-red patent stilettos

worn all day at the office with matching lipstick smile
and that tailored grey suit she squeezed herself into

first thing, as if kitting up for a scuba-dive.
Yet she strides along the street like a military model

on the catwalk, each clipped step clicked into place
on the spot, just-so. Blisters pucker in the vees

of those pointed toes; heels chafe and swell,
tender as pancetta; soles sweat in the steep

curve of the shank; but she walks with such an air
as if the shoes are leading the legs in a devil's dance.

Beware, beware. An ankle will twist
and sprain, a tendon rip, a metatarsal snap,

and you'll never make it to the end of the path.
But here she stops, leans on the rail and off

they go, one by one, slapped together
like a pair of red snapper and packed in her bag

and out come her trainers – pink as peonies, pink
as raspberries, pink as a galah cockatoo.

When she slips them on, she's four inches shorter,
feet on the ground, and away she flies.

Hat

Whatever is it doing there, lying all forlorn
   in the gutter as if it's slipped from the crown
of the lopsided moon? Whoever would have cast
   it off unwanted this early side of midnight,
such a doodle-dandy, such a beau chapeau
   as this, with its broad brim and silver trim,
this pink, ten-gallon cowboy hat?
   Was it hurled to the kerb in a fury of tears
by some dishevelled, Wild West party reveller
   flaunting her all in weskit, shorts and boots
as she watched her pal make off with her catch?
   Or did a posse of lads, out on the town,
snatch it for a laugh from a theme-bar hostess
   to play frisbee in the street in a maul of torsos
and *Yee-haas!* as it spun towards the stars?
   Did it slowly slide down the waterfall
of hair of a girl with her neck arched back,
   wrapped in shadow, lost in a kiss?
Without a head to tip or tilt it, to doff or swagger off,
   it's a hat without a heart. Flapping
on the ground in the breeze, it lifts and gulps,
   a lolling tongue, an open mouth,
its drawstring trailing in the wet, a noose of desire.

Making a Herringbone Harris Tweed Garment

She sews the black and grey, the dye
    of the minke whale, the sloe, the cormorant's wing,
        wave, machair and sky
the weaver wove from the yarn

She sews the black and grey and blue, the dye
    of the mussel-bed, the myrtle, the kittiwake,
        wave, machair and sky
the weaver wove from the yarn of the weft

She sews the black and grey, the blue and orange, the dye
    of the skate, the autumn fingers of apricot club, the painted lady,
        wave, machair and sky
the weaver wove from the yarn of weft and warp

She sews the black and grey, the blue and orange and brown, the dye
    of the kelp, the leaves and bark of the birch, the corncrake,
        wave, machair and sky
the weaver wove from the yarn of weft and warp on the beam

She sews the black and grey, the blue, the orange and brown and red,
        the dye
    of the starfish washed up on the shore, the crottle, the damselfly,
        wave, machair and sky
the weaver wove from the yarn of weft and warp on the beam and loom

She sews the black and grey, the blue and orange, the brown and red
        and green, the dye
    of the crab in the bladderwrack, the blossoming broom,
               the lapwing's plumage,
        wave, machair and sky
the weaver wove from the yarn of weft and warp on the beam and loom
        in his croft

She sews the black and grey, the blue, orange and brown, the red
and green and white, the dye
of the windswept dune, the mountain hare in its winter coat,
the cirrus clouds,
wave, machair and sky
the weaver wove from the yarn of weft and warp on the beam and loom
in his croft
on the outer isle

Bow-tie

There are some who come in here haven't got
a clue. When I offer one to him, he looks as if
I'm placing an octopus in his hands, both ends
dangling like silk tentacles. I restrain a smile
as he turns to the mirror and strikes a pose:
below the lifted jaw, his stubby thumbs
and fingers fumble the ribbon like a fan-belt
that needs changing. He grips and twists and tugs
and ends up with a trussed fist tight against
his throat, a plucked capon. A fine garrotte
but not, definitely not, a knot. As he gawps
at me for help, I pretend to fold a shirt.
His gnarled finger-nails give him away: if I show
him how, he'll never remember. I purse my lips
and suggest a simpler style. After all, it's just
a one-off occasion, sir. A hook and elasticated
clasp will do the trick. Or better still,
a clip-on piece that clings to the shirt like a drooping
moustache. So easily pleased with my advice, he'll take
the cuff-links, cummerbund and silver armbands, too.
Wants to look the part. Indeed you do, sir.
Indeed you do.

Early Sun

It always comes this time of year
when we've all got used to weather
damp and heavy as a khaki greatcoat –
a dazzling tinfoil day arrives

out of the blue in sheets of light,
freeing the lustre from every surface.
The Avon's muddiness is spinning
silver along its six mile rush

to the sea as if some muscular moon
is working overtime at the loom.
Runners dash at you from every
direction, no longer muffled shadows

panting plumes of breath into the grey
but striding out in bright vests,
nudging past every pedestrian
taking a stroll along the footpath.

And look, the walkers are cutting a spritely
pace, too, in sunglasses and smiles: their hands
are out of their pockets and scribbling the gist
of their stories to their fresh-faced families –

or clutching the shoulder of this afternoon's
lover, a brace of bodies held close
with the heat beneath their coats.
Everyone knows it's a false Spring

that slips from the grasp like a mirror's reflection.
Even the pair of gleaming spaniels
trotting across the park with their snouts
in the air are aware they'll be back on the leash

soon as the rays start to fade. Above
the perimeter wall, a row of cherries
has broken into blossom: pink
nebulae hanging in their bronze spheres.

A Grandfather Dancing with a Child on his Shoulders

Hey Grandad, is that a spot
of Fred-and-Ginger footwork
you're tapping out on the pavement,
or the hop/hop-back of an Irish jig
with your hands aloft round the legs
of the bouncing, giggling child?
Or is it an old salt's hornpipe,
performed on the quay to the flute
and fiddle in your head? Is that
light-footed 4/4 skip a step
you've practised in the sycamore
soles of your clogs to make the boy
gasp at your mazurka spin?
And are you bearded Zorba now,
rising and dipping on the beach
to the bouzouki beat of the waves?
Those swaying hips, that swing
and stretch of leg and toe, can only be a tango
to bandoneon that puts the lad at ease.
What comes next in your repertoire?
Calypso, cucaracha or the Lambeth Walk?
Minuet, moonwalk, waltz? Or are you
ready, ready, ready to rock'n'roll?
And as for the toddler who sits like an exotic
head-dress, he's learning the art
of balance, Grandad, while you kick
and swirl your carnival dance in the sun.

A Bunch of Fives

I wanted to be a boxer once, says Az,
opening the blade, testing it on his thumb.
Reflected in the mirror, de Niro's photo
stands on guard: gloves clenched at his chin,
he stares from Jake la Motta's bullish eyes.

A dozen fights, he recalls, *and I won them all.*
As the razor trims the bristles on my cheek,
Bruce Lee's poised to take on Mr Han:
focused Shaolin gaze, a groove in the brow;
arms and hands outstretched like dragon's wings.

But my father made me choose at seventeen.
He nicks at the curve of beard across my throat
as Michael Caine strikes a deal with Altabani
in the Alps: his Charlie Croker's suave as a lynx
in that white polo-neck, his claws concealed.

*Barber or boxer, my Papa said, but your hands
aren't made for both*, and he snips the fringe of hairs
on my lip while Eastwood peers from the shade of his fedora:
The Man with No Name chews a cheroot,
scheming the fistful of dollars he'll do without.

They're not my idols, says Az, *except for him*,
and he points at the snap of Ali on the wall
acting the clown before the Cooper fight:
the fan of fingers, his oracle mouth predicting five.
He's the only real man amongst them all.

Mmenson

after Edward Kamau Brathwaite

Summon now the king of the air,
the chopper's rotor roaring,
the throbbing drum of the skies.

Rouse the commanders-in-chief, princes of the provinces,
sleeping in their compounds, dreaming in their bunkers; raise
the advance columns, the bomb-disposal units, the outriders
                                        flying like eagles.

Broadcast now the gains and losses:
the toll of military casualties, the critical, the wounded;
tally the enemy fatalities (avoid civilian statistics), the captives

and scroll down the CGIs of battlefields, aerial bombardments,
armoured brigades and sniper-fire. Roar copter, raptor
                        circling the villages,
blades scything the carcass of the land –

land of the beginning, land of knowledge,
tablet, stylus, cuneiform, land of hanging gardens and ziggurat,
land of Marduk, Nabu, Sin, Shamash, Ishtar.

Fire the elephant horn of your L30 120mm tank gun. Roll-call
        the corpses, airlifted home;
bugle the solemn bystanders; drape the flags on the coffin-parade
in a Wiltshire town, where a white horse whinnies on the hill.

Car

Not content – and who would be? –
with the classic, limited edition, black
2 litre BMW convertible
he keeps at his holiday-home in Italy
for cruising the winding roads
between the vineyards and olive-groves
of Le Marché – foot down on the straight,
easing into the bends with the lightest
touch on the wheel, every bit
the rally-driver manqué or would-be star
of some black-and-white Pasolini movie –
my friend Geoff, from Mansfield,
wants a Maserati. He's set his sights
on it, his sole unquenchable desire: to be
a streamlined blaze hitting the autostrada
between the mountains and the sea
at 200 kilometres an hour.

                        And yet
the trouble is he can't decide between
a silver coupe Gran Turismo
with 4.2 V8 cylinders
and 0–60 in 4.65 seconds,
or the Trident MC12 in white
and blue livery with creamy leather
upholstery and god-knows-what-size
engine.

      Geoff, I tell him over a beer,
looking him squarely in the eye,
Geoff, I understand your problem.

Man in a Mustang

Why else would I be sitting here parked on double-yellow lines
in the centre of town on a bright and busy Saturday morning,
elbow resting on the sill, one hand lolling on the wheel, the other

easing through my hair as I lean back in the seat, if it weren't for
that moment I started coming round in the ward, my eyes still shut –
as they are now behind my shades – against the intensity of light

in the world, though I wasn't sure which world it emanated from
or which soft white world I was lying in? And I knew that after
three coronaries and the fourth off-stage, a shadow in the wings,

that there's only now to play for and the script's in my hands.
Dreams have wheels, are chrome-trimmed, convertible.
So I flew out West, bought this sky-blue '65 and took the road-trip.

Sounds like some delayed adolescent Dean Moriarty fantasy, you say?
Why not, say I, my eyes on the dials. Cruising Route 66
                                        with the top down,
girlfriend by my side, and music on the radio – the stations changing

as we crossed the county-lines. The miles streamed like arterial blood
to the V8 pulse along those highways, from LA to Albuquerque
and Oklahoma, up to Illinois then east to NYC to ship this baby home.

See that badge on the grille? The silver pony gleaming in the sun
– its neck straining, scissor-legs slicing the air, tail flying and every
                                        sinew at full stretch.
Its hooves are pounding, systole and diastole, and I'm riding it. Riding.

On the M4 in the Inside Lane

And I find myself cruising in a truck's slipstream,
trying to count the pallets on its juddering trailer –
1, 2 … 4, 5 … must be 10 to a stack, I guess –
as we ride the camber and undulations of the road
and I try to calculate how many are roped up there
in the entire load

                    – like Chris and I would do
after going flat-out for an hour at the bench
and taking a breather to wait for Steve the Forklift
to clear the floor. We'd lay the nail-guns on the jig,
push back our masks and muffs, and stand there
wiping the dust from our lips, figuring our output.

We needed the down-time. We knew exactly how many
we had to assemble to earn some bonus. Didn't care
where they went or what they carried, so long as
we raked it in. Time and motion topped our wages up
so we logged every minute of stoppage

                    – must be two hundred
on their way to some depot or yard – that's half of what
we could knock up in a shift, nailing the boards and slats
to the blocks then swinging the decks in sync to stacks
of ten. As I pull out to overtake, there's a waft of timber
and sweat. On the wheel, my hands are soft as bank-notes.

Although the Woodlouse

is a creature of the dark and damp, another one crawls out
      of some crevice to make its Marco Polo
progress across the flat-earth floorboards between
      the hearth and rug towards … Does it even
know its destination, this glossy, hump-backed island
      of insouciance? Out there, it's no high-plains drifter,
alone on the timber highway and threatening menace
      with each spur-clinking step. No Maoist proletarian
ant on a mission. No camouflaged stick-insect going
      with the grain. It's one on its own, out on its own.
It creeps out of hiding and makes itself at home. From a mite's
      eye view, it might appear an armour-plated
articulated war-machine enamoured of destruction,
      its radar on red alert; or with bossed flanks,
head-down and snorting, some comic-book creature primed
      for the charge. But lift a brick or log in the garden
to expose a nest of them, they're all at odds, belly-up,
      their fourteen legs and antennae twitching,
or curled into crusty pods, playing dead. And this one,
      meanwhile, saunters along its route, pauses
to take the lie of the land and hopes to pass unseen,
      leaving no trail, this anonymous isopod,
thick-skinned flâneur, dreaming of cosy composting retreats.

Knocking Up a Garden Planter

One of those jobs I left to decompose
in the mind, dumped the timber in a corner
of the shed. But today its design and dimensions
are honed like a blade on a stone and I set to work.

The saw bites its rhythm along the line, frets
the grain in a spray of dust and scorching fibre
till off-cuts clatter to the ground. A chippy
would opt for clamps, chiselled or chamfered joints.

Not me. I go for the whir and whine of the drill,
wrench the screws to butt the ends in place.
The wood can writhe for all its worth to pull
itself awry and sit askew, I'll not give in.

It's shaping up with rough precision. Give
or take, the sides align a few degrees
from square. A base that almost fits. Legs
that wobble to the touch. It'll do.

Packed with compost, soon it will fill
with mint and parsley, chives and dill.

Occasion

Easing your hand
sideways–on
between the raspy
canes and into
the canopy of pale
green light

you twist and lift
your wrist beneath
the curling, curative
trusses of leaves
as if practising
a magician's gesture

in search of *rubus
idaeus* – as Ida
did for infant Zeus,
the drops of blood
from her pricked breast
soaking the white berries

forever red –
as now, with palm
cupped, closing
your finger–tips
round the ruby
drupelets, you pull

away, unhasping
the fruit from its plug,
the rich juices
drizzling your skin
with the same traces
which, offered up,

imprint my lips,
sweet on the tongue.

Rhubarb

Broad fans of plumage plucked
from some mythic bird the hunters trekked
the snow-capped hills to track,

the leathery crinkled leaves you snap
from the stems. Fresh from the plot, stalks
of emerald sheen and ruby veins

lie on the kitchen-table like tribal
instruments set out for the priest
to let the ceremonial blood.

They wait for the knife to trim and chop
across the grooves, prepare them
for the sugar coating and the hob.

In dynastic China they were used to cure
the plague. Along the Silk Road,
valued with diamonds, musk and pearls.

Bringing your harvest home from the allotment,
you told me how as a child you'd tie
the leaves to your arms and try to fly.

Blackberries in August

You brush aside convolvulus
and mistletoe, stretch beyond
the nettles to the floricanes,
and lift the cluster of leaves

to find the secret hoard,
black globes hanging by a thread,
each one a constellation
of dark stars glancing light,

and you feel that yours is the hand
of a god cupped beneath one,
then two, then a glut of them,
as they freely come away

plump in your grasp, the juice
oozing, seeping into the skin
of your palm, fresh blood
along its convoluted lines.

Sanctuary

Cantilevered necks, muzzles scrunched
in straw, a dozen chomping donkeys stand

rigid in a circle round a spilled bale.
Spines gnarled and bowed, their tails droop,

flags of defeat. They're eating out their days
with eyes shut against the old burdens:

over-laden carts and panniers, open
wounds, founder, the whip burning the flank.

At the edge of the field, a lone donkey lifts
its head and brays a curse against the world.

Ash

The watching starts at this time
of year when the first buds appear,
black jewels clustered on every
branch of its platinum February crown.

I'm keeping an eye on the bark
for lesions in its leathery olive skin,
for tell-tale scars of purple rust
where spores would be bedding in,

brought on a sharp east wind
when the south-westerly relents.
Unscathed for now, its lithe branches
swaying, stretching towards the sun,

my Yggdrasil stands deep-rooted
at the centre of the world. Always last
to leaf, it only takes a few
bright days in May for its flowers

to burst into a sphere of green fire.
Its leaves can conjure lovers to a lover's
dreams and in its glinting canopy
the blackbird sings all summer.

Pillbox

Twenty thousand dawns I've watched
the shudder of light on the meandering waters,
the reeds on standby for the valley's invasions.

Waiting for the drone of raiding aircraft,
I've spotted the hawk high over Hindover,
hanging its threat from an invisible tripwire.

Listening for the boom on the foreshore, the thud
between the breaking waves, I've heard
the landing-craft of swans cruising upstream.

Watching for the shadow on the hills, the dark cross
slipping in and out of cloud, I've glimpsed
a glint of heron's beak, lone sniper in the reeds.

Twenty thousand dawns I've waited:
wind in the hawthorn, elder, chestnut;
light shaking the cowslips, trembling the silverweed.

Observation Post

Our sources have reported nocturnal sightings
just beyond the city limits: a glimpse of moonlit eyes,
scurrying shadows, tracks in the soil. We've gathered
data to plot the route. From Dundry Hill and Harptree
and further into the Mendips – wherever they retreated
when we poisoned their territory more years ago
than anyone can recall – they're making incursions
through Hanging Hill Wood. They bivvy up by day
in roots of oak and alder; venture out under cover
of brambles, nettles, bugloss and deepest night
to the water's edge. What is it that brings them back?
Revenge or plunder? A colonisation instinct or a fragile
alliance? To attribute these is to see ourselves in their eyes.

Let's say they simply sniff the velvet green-black air
and go with the prevailing wind as they launch and glide
down Colliter's Brook. We're lying in wait for their return.
Our night-vision technology monitors the advance
of sleek snouts, eyes, ears rippling the surface.
We lose them when they arch their backs and dive.
Submerged, they're glossy ghosts that stalk our fears.
When they leap onto the bank they trip the infra-reds,
are caught in the flash: muscular haunches, spiky pelts,
the returned gaze. To verify their presence, we collect
their spraints as they drag their tails to the water. *Lutra lutra*,
paused on the margin. What do they leave? Webbed prints
already faint, drying. The scent of fish and hay.

Unknown

whether
        it's just this moment arrived
        leaping along the boundary
        of wood and open field
        its trail of prints incised
        by strides of twice its length
and come to a halt

or if
        it's been here all along
        at the edge of light and dark
        damp pelted, hooves
        pressing leaves to mould
        ears alert to the frisson
of footsteps pausing

but what it is
        this crossing of paths
        as we catch each other's
        scent is a pact of stillness
        at a distance, waiting to see
        eye to eye
in the mist

White Horse in a Snowfield

It's as if the field is all sky, the sky all field,
    as if the horse is all field, all sky.

A fluster of snowflakes is a plume of horse-breath;
    a drift of mist, the slow swish of its tail.

Beneath its gelid coat, earth's muscles and arteries
    freeze, its bones compact of ice.

It could be a creature hewn from limestone on a hill,
    or waiting for Rhiannon, frost-maned,

sculpted and spectral, a space on a page. The horizon's
    erased in a white-out of air; the horse

coralled in a blizzard that's closing the world down.

Polar

balanced
on this thin tier
like a ballerina on a birthday-cake
posed
on hind legs
on this floe the shape of a reflected cloud
(for the man on the ship
who'll post
his JPGs on the web
and tag
No Room for Nanook
on Arctic Isle)
nose in the air
to catch
a whiff of seal's breath
I'm a whalebone-sketch
on the wall
of a chamber seen by torchlight
and my claws
incise the ice
my paws imprint their butterfly wings
in the melt
of my final stand

Tree Gatherer

Lorenzo Pellegrini, Risoud Forest, Jura

When he embraces the spruce, trunk
to trunk – his arms straining to circle
its girth, his breath in time to its breath,
his heart an echo of its inner pulse –
he gazes up at its green spire
twisting into the canopy, his ear
pressed to the scales of its bark, and hears
the wind fretting its branches, the sap
seeping from its roots into the soil,
the resonance of every ring in its flesh
vibrating like a string on a sound-board
across the centuries of growth,
and he knows that this is the one to choose.

The day of the lowest moon, he's ready
to fell. He tests the precision of teeth
on the chain. Buzzes the notch. Bores
into the fibres until it's balanced
for a moment on a hinge, like a violin
held between neck and wrist,
before he drives the bow of his saw
into the cut and hits the crescendo.
The slow topple of timber. A column
of silence scrolls the air. And when
it lies at rest, he rolls his hand
across the grain, feeling its stave
inscribed with signature and clef.

Afon Rhymni

There's no river like your first river
Down the years of your life, it rolls forever
At the end of Ball Lane you hear its call
From the hills to the sea, it flows and falls

There's no river like your first river
From the Beacons to the Channel, it rolls forever
At the end of Ball Lane it flows and falls
From Rhymney to the Lambies, you hear its call

There's no river like your first river
From Llanbradach to Llanrumney, it rolls forever
At the end of Ball Lane you hear its call
From Ystrad Mynach to Machen it flows and falls

There's no river like your first river
From Bedwas to Draethen it rolls forever
At the end of Ball Lane it flows and falls
From Bargoed to Rumney, you hear its call

There's no river like your first river
Down the years of your life, it rolls forever
At the end of Ball Lane you hear its call
From the hills to the sea, it flows and falls

Footpath, Cardigan Bay

All afternoon the waves have been racing ahead
of us, their fractured ribs now glinting, now
shadowed by cloud. However much we scan
the rise and fall of the track we follow or study
our footing as we climb the stiles, it draws our gaze,
the sea, it draws our gaze beyond the bronze
bracken and the last flickering flames of gorse
on the bent-back cliffs scaling down to the coves
below. And suddenly a pair of kites
soar up from below our sightline. They ride the air,
every feather a gleam of light as they wheel and drift
above us and we stand, heads craned, all eyes.

Langland Bay: Morning

Alfred Sisley (1897)

He must have gone down that morning
        from the Osborne Hotel to a bay
of brimming light. With brushes, canvas, oils,
        he went prepared to take it all in,
the sky's and sea's transparency.

But this was not the lustre of the Seine,
        its shimmering reflections of orchards,
willows, mills, quays. Here there was no sweep
        of burnished gold across the fields;
no trembling glint of poplar avenues.

The beach where he stood opened out
        onto the illimitable. It caught his breath
and he coughed, hacking the air. The sky, as always
        to his eyes, was lilac softness
between the clouds. Yet at the meeting-point

the sea incised its cobalt edge –
        as if the waves had pared away
the flush of colour to this blue opaque:
        tintless, dense enough to press,
prod and drag across the palette.

He'd seen the waters rise at Moret;
        depicted, in choppy flecks, the floods
at Port-Marly – the slosh of overflow
        against aqueduct and bridge,
the meadows streaming with swirls of grey.

But here the rollers' shoreward drive
        out of that impenetrable line
released a rush and flow of brush-strokes
        across the expanse, loosely pluming,
the highlights twisting their comets' tails.

And at the centre, solid between shadows of land,
　　　　Storr's Rock. Its black asperities,
foam-sprayed, broke the waves, dragged
　　　　the ocean's surge into its fissures:
raspy concretion of the undercurrent dark.

The wind skimmed its blade across the cove.
　　　　Again he coughed, easing the tumour
in the throat. He felt the give and resistance
　　　　of canvas on the frame, and on the brush
the black-tipped bristle, fragile in the light.

Acknowledgements

Several of these poems first appeared in my chapbook, *Waiting for the Wave* (Brighton: Pighog Press, 2012) and I am very grateful to the editor, John Davies, for his support and encouragement in that venture.

A few other poems were first published in *The Cardiff Review, Raceme* and *Stony Thursday.* My thanks go to the editors of those journals.

'The Poet of the Mason's Arms' was written for the John Tripp Memorial Night in Bargoed, March 2015, organised by Julie Pritchard.

'Where' was written as part of *Seven Stars*, a poetry sequence produced and performed by The Spoke, with live music by Eyebrow, in the Sanctum project, curated by Theaster Gates in Bristol, 2015.

The Spoke is the poetry workshop-&-performance group in which I am fortunate to be a member. The 'tough love' advice and enthusiasm of the other members of the group – Elizabeth Parker, Claire Williamson and Paul Deaton – has been invaluable to me in the writing and live reading of most poems in this collection.

My thanks to Jeff Schlanger, the amazing performance painter and musicWitness to jazz in New York City. Our chance encounter brought jazz, art and poetry into an exciting collaboration. You can see more of Jeff's work on www.musicwitness.com.

I am grateful to my editor, Amy Wack, for her unfailing energy and for encouraging me to put this collection together and submit it to Seren. Many of the poems received their first airing at Seren's wonderful First Thursday of the Month at Chapter Arts Centre event organised by Amy.